# Embroidery Machine
## ESSENTIALS

## Basic Techniques

## 20 Designs and Project Ideas to Develop Your Embroidery Skills

# By Jeanine Twigg

Published by

**krause
publications**

700 East State Street • Iola, WI 54990-0001

Please call or write for our free catalog of publications. Our toll-free number, to place an order or to obtain a free catalog, is 800-258-0929. Please use our regular business telephone 715-445-2214 for editorial comment and further information.

ISBN: 0-87349-580-2

**Copyright Information for Embroidery Designs on the CD-ROM:**

Project Manager: Jeanine Twigg
Illustrations and layout: Melinda Bylow
Design digitizing: Craig Dunmore

# Table of Contents

# Introduction

The *Embroidery Machine Essentials*: *Companion Project Series* was created to provide you with decorative designs and creative uses to help develop your embroidery skills. Through this series you'll discover ways of looking beyond the "face value" of a design to recognize its creative potential. Once you've discovered a variety of techniques that can be used with even your most simplistic designs, you'll begin to look at every decorative design with an entirely new creative approach.

The 20 embroidery designs included on the accompanying CD-ROM have been created especially for this book – you cannot get them anywhere else. While the designs are visually simple, the technique appeal is tremendous. You'll be amazed at what you can do with 20 designs that encompass over 65 stitch variations.

There are designs within designs that can be used for a variety of basic embroidery techniques. Additional stops were specifically digitized into the designs to offer additional creative potential. For example, within the Circles (Satin) — each circle represents a different size appliqué that can be used for Traditional Appliqué, Fleece Appliqué, Reverse Appliqué and more. You'll be amazing how many different ways a circle can be used in

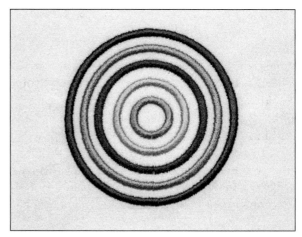

*Circles (Satin)*

embroidery. The shape is simple but the ideas for use will offer the practice you need to develop your embroidery skills. Instead of having six separate design files, one for each circle, we combined the design for compact embroidery convenience. If you prefer, most of the designs can be split up into individual files. Simply use a design editing software to break up the designs and save the individual designs in separate files.

Have fun experimenting with these basic techniques and be sure to keep *Embroidery Machine Essentials* by your side every step of the way!

Your embroidery friend,

*Jeanine*

**With appreciation:** I'd like to thank Melinda for the awesome illustrations, fashion drawings, and layout of the book, Craig Dunmore for the digitizing of the designs, and my family, friends and colleagues for their patience and understanding during the coordination of this series. In addition, this book would not be possible without the generosity of the companies whose contributions of equipment, software, and support were used to create the samples that fill the pages of this book. See Resources on page 47.

# Chapter 1
# Embroidery Essentials

First and foremost, be sure to keep a copy of *Embroidery Machine Essentials* by your side as you work through the techniques in this book. The comprehensive embroidery information found in *Embroidery Machine Essentials* will help with the basics of how to hoop, stabilize and stitch decorative designs. It will be referred to as a source for obtaining basic embroidery instructions for the completion of some techniques.

## Embroidery Designs

The embroidery designs, featured in this book, are located on the CD-ROM on the inside back cover. You must have a computer and compatible embroidery software to access and utilize the decorative designs. Basic computer knowledge will be helpful to understand how to copy the designs onto the hard drive of your computer.

To access the designs, insert the CD-ROM into your computer. The designs are located on the CD-ROM in folders for each embroidery machine format. Copy the design files onto the hard drive of your computer using one of the operating system programs or open the designs directly into applicable embroidery software. Be sure to copy only the design format compatible with your brand of embroidery equipment.

Once the designs are in your embroidery software or saved on your computer, transfer the designs to your embroidery machine following the manufacturer's instructions for the equipment. For more information about using these designs with your software or embroidery equipment, consult your owner's manual or seek advice from the dealer that honors your equipment warranty.

## Copyright

The 20 embroidery designs on the CD-ROM are unique. You cannot obtain these designs anywhere except with the purchase of this book. Please be faithful to the copyright laws that govern embroidery designs. In other words, be honest. It is illegal to share, trade, copy or sell any embroidery design. For more information on the copyright laws that govern embroidery designs, visit **www.embroideryprotection.com** on the Internet.

You may embroider the designs for your personal use and on items for resale or gifts. Respect of the copyright laws protects the designers and thereby assures a steady supply of original designs with high quality digitizing and standards.

## Design Segments

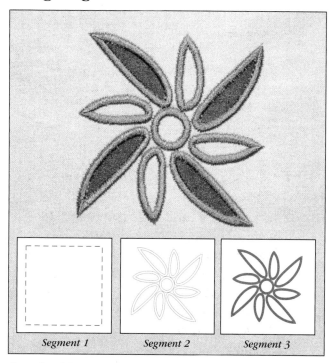

*Sample of Cutwork Flower and stitch segments*

Each design provided with this book was digitized with additional stops to accommodate a variety of techniques that can be stitched within each design. These additional stops are referred to as "segments." Every time the embroidery machine stops it is considered the end of a segment. It may not necessarily mean that a thread change is needed. A listing of the segments and recommended colors for each design is located in the Appendix starting on page 43.

In addition, a full-size image of each design along with the individual segments can be found in PDF (Portable Document Format) files on the CD-ROM. Adobe Acrobat Reader version 5.0 or higher will be required to view and print these files. This software is available on the CD-ROM for your convenience.

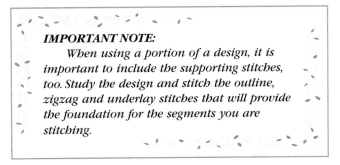

**IMPORTANT NOTE:**
*When using a portion of a design, it is important to include the supporting stitches, too. Study the design and stitch the outline, zigzag and underlay stitches that will provide the foundation for the segments you are stitching.*

### Perimeter Baste

Another unique feature built in to each design is a design perimeter baste (segment 1). These long stitches will hold the fabric and stabilizer layers together during the embroidery process. The perimeter baste also provides an approximate design size that will aid in the placement of appliqué fabrics.

The first color of every design is black to represent the perimeter baste feature. It is not necessary to use black thread, rather use the color that will be used to stitch segment 2 to avoid unnecessary thread changes. If your machine already has a basting stitch feature, skip segment 1 and use the machine's perimeter baste or edit out segment 1 using a stitch editing software.

The perimeter baste is quick and easy to remove after the embroidery process. On the backside of the embroidery before unhooping the fabric, snip the basting stitch threads about every 3-4 stitches. Then, on the top of fabric in one of the corners, pull up on

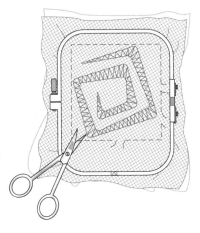

the top basting thread to remove the stitches. The clipped bobbin threads will poke up on top of the fabric and can be removed easily.

### Test-Stitching

The test stitching of any design is one of the most important steps of the embroidery process. Thoroughly test-stitch designs onto fabric the same or similar to that of the item to be embroidered to determine if the correct stabilizer, thread, needle and design is being used for the project. Be sure to pre-wash any item and test-stitch fabric to be embroidered.

Use the test-stitch process to practice the step-by-step techniques in this book. Then, keep the test-stitch samples in a notebook with notes and comments for future reference.

### Thread Colors

At the end of each segment, the embroidery machine will stop indicating a color change or the end of the design. The Appendix: Design Details, found on page 43, provides a picture of the individual segments within each design. The colors listed are only suggested thread colors — let your personal preference be your guide to color selection. The thread colors that appear on your embroidery machine may not necessarily represent the color thread that should be used. Each embroidery machine is different in the way thread colors and designs are displayed. These Design Details are also available for printing from the CD-ROM in order to have a color guide by your side while stitching the techniques. Print this file using a color printer for best results.

## Embroidery Supplies

Each technique or project will require some basic embroidery supplies. Refer to *Embroidery Machine Essentials* for comprehensive information about the basics of embroidery. Here's a refresher pertinent to this book.

### Stabilizers

There are three types of stabilizers — cut-away, tear-away and disappearing. Cut-away stabilizers are permanent and are cut away from the outside edge of the embroidery design after the

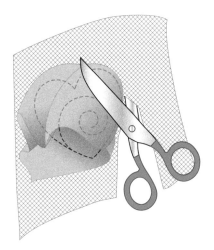

embroidery process. The stabilizer will remain intact through the laundry process and is mostly used with dense designs and fabrics that stretch.

Tear-away stabilizers are temporary and are torn away from the outside edge of the embroidery after the embroidery process. The fabric must support the embroidery stitches with minimal aid from the stabilizer as it disappears over time in the laundry process.

Disappearing stabilizers are those that are removed with water or the heat of an iron. The water-soluble varieties are 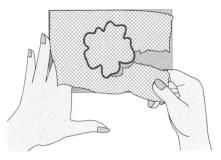 mostly used on top of the fabric, but are also available in a heavier form for use as a backing. Stabilizers that are removed with the heat of an iron must be used with fabric that can tolerate this method. Both types of disappearing stabilizers must be used with fabric that can support the weight of the embroidery design without added assistance from the stabilizer.

### Temporary Spray Adhesives

Temporary spray adhesives are an integral part of the embroidery process. A can of temporary spray adhesive, specifically designed for embroidery, can be used to secure an appliqué layer to a base fabric, help tame slippery fabrics and secure a base fabric to a hooped stabilizer. Be sure to spray away from the embroidery machine, as the overspray can be harmful to the equipment.

### Scissors

Curved, double curved, appliqué and paper-cutting scissors are perfect to have on hand for the embroidery process. Use curved embroidery scissors to snip threads and to cut closely to appliqué fabrics. Use double curved embroidery scissors to snip threads while the fabric is hooped and attached to the embroidery machine. Use appliqué scissors to trim appliqué edges on fleece. Be sure to use paper-only scissors to cut stabilizers as to not dull fabric cutting scissors.

### Needles & Threads

Needle sizes and types will vary depending on the fabric used for the individual techniques or project ideas. Metallic threads should always be used with a needle manufactured specifically for use with metallic threads. For best results, follow your sewing knowledge when it comes to choosing needles for embroidery. For example, use a blunt end needle for knit fabrics and a sharp point needle for woven fabrics.

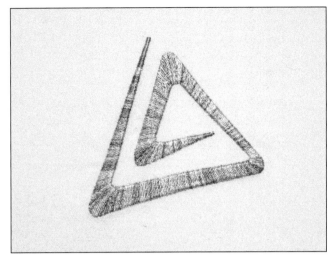

*Retro Triangle with variegated thread*

When it comes to thread, allow your personal preference to be your guide. Some like cotton, some like rayon, some like polyester and some like them all! The designs on the accompanying CD-ROM were digitized for 40-weight thread. Enlarge the designs to accommodate a heavier thread. The designs will accommodate a lighter thread without changing the design size. Use a polyester or acrylic thread for items that will be washed frequently. Use a rayon or metallic thread for embroidered items that are for show, washed infrequently or dry-cleaned. And, use an appropriate size needle to accommodate both the fabric and the thread.

### Hooping

Use the smallest size hoop to accommodate the design to be embroidered. Once the fabric is hooped, do not pull or tug on the fabric. Tighten the screw on the hoop only during the hooping trial period. Hoop and unhoop the fabric until the correct tension is achieved. Tugging on the fabric after the fabric is in the hoop will result in puckers around the design once the fabric is removed from the hoop.

# Chapter 2
# Appliqué

 ne of the easiest ways to eliminate excess stitches and save time at the embroidery machine is to use an appliqué. The idea is simple – apply one fabric to the surface of another with decorative stitching. Industry expert, Mary Mulari, refers to embroidery machine appliqué as "automatic appliqué" — the embroidery machine does most of the work for you!

A variety of fabrics can be used for appliqué. Some lightweight or knit fabrics should be interfaced before the appliqué process to help support the weight of the stitches. Using a heavy appliqué fabric on a light base fabric will cause the appliqué to droop. Therefore, choose fabrics that are compatible in weight with the base fabric.

There are several popular edge finishes for appliqué. A Satin Stitch edge finish is classic, a Blanket Stitch edge finish is traditional, and a simple Outline Stitch is the finish of choice for fabrics that do not ravel. The type of fabric used for the appliqué will determine the appropriate edge finish. For more information about Appliqué, refer to pages 57-60 in *Embroidery Machine Essentials*.

## Stitch & Trim Appliqué

*Appliqué Flower*

This method is by far the easiest of the appliqué methods and is usually embroidered with a Satin Stitch edge finish. Precision is needed for the trimming of the appliqué fabric close to the outline stitch. Lift up on the excess fabric and trim closely with a curved embroidery scissors. When using

appliqué designs from another source, be sure to test-stitch the designs using this method. It may be necessary to use a template for the appliqué shape to keep from having fabric edges poke out from under the Satin Stitch edge finish.

**Instructions:**

1. Mark the placement of the design and hoop the base fabric with a stabilizer appropriate for the base fabric. Place the hoop on the machine and stitch segment 1 (perimeter baste) of the Appliqué Flower.

2. Cut a piece of appliqué fabric slightly larger than the perimeter baste. Lightly spray the back of the fabric with temporary adhesive and secure the piece to the base fabric while the hoop is still on the machine.

3. Stitch segment 2 (flower outline). Remove the hoop from the machine; do not remove the fabric from the hoop. Use a sharp curved tip scissors or appliqué scissors to trim around the outside edge of the outline. Trim the fabric within 1/8" or less from the stitches for best results.

4. Return the hoop to the machine and stitch the remaining design.

*Designs that can be used for this technique:*

## *Template Appliqué*

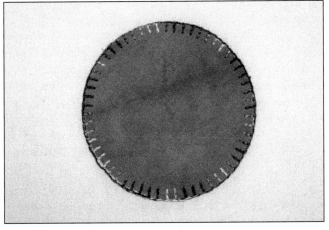

*Segments 6 and 7 of Circles (Blanket)*

This method requires the use of templates to make the appliqué fabric the exact size of the Circles (Blanket) stitch design. There are several methods of making templates — refer to page 57 of *Embroidery Machine Essentials* for detailed instructions.

### Instructions:

1. Make a circle template by stitching segments 2, 4, 6, 8 or 10 (outline) with black thread on white fabric. Then, make a photocopy of the fabric and cut out the circle from the copy to use as a template. Or, stitch segment 2, 4, 6, 8 or 10 (outline) onto an index card taped to the back of the hoop and cut out the circle.

2. Trace the template(s) directly onto the back of an appliqué fabric, an interfaced appliqué fabric, or a press-sensitive/fusible web backed appliqué fabric. Cut out the shapes.

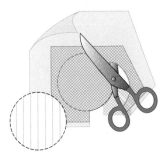

3. Mark the placement of the design and hoop the base fabric with the appropriate stabilizer for the fabric. Place the hoop on the machine, stitch segment 1 (perimeter baste) of the Circles (Blanket) and segment 6 (or any one of the outlines in the design).

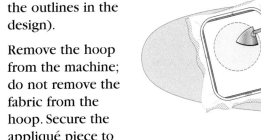

4. Remove the hoop from the machine; do not remove the fabric from the hoop. Secure the appliqué piece to the base fabric with a temporary spray adhesive, a mini-iron or pressure.

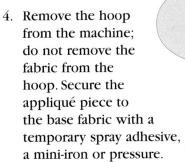

5. Return the hoop to the machine and stitch segment 7 (blanket stitch) or the blanket stitch number that comes after the outline stitched in Step 3.

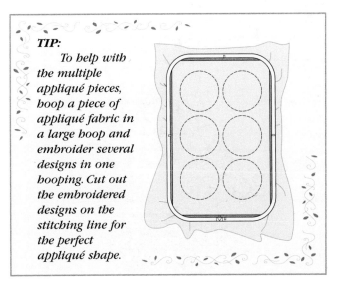

*TIP:*
To help with the multiple appliqué pieces, hoop a piece of appliqué fabric in a large hoop and embroider several designs in one hooping. Cut out the embroidered designs on the stitching line for the perfect appliqué shape.

## Sheer Appliqué

*Heart*

Add a bit of sheer elegance to any design with organza. Organza is a sheer nylon or polyester fabric that has a variety of finishes — from sparkle to a hint of color.

Hoop the base fabric with the appropriate stabilizer. Cut a piece (or several pieces) of organza 5" square and secure the layer(s) to the hooped fabric with segment 1 (perimeter baste). Embroider directly over sheer organza, remove perimeter basting stitches, and trim away the fabric close to the stitching after the satin stitch finish.

To remove the sheer fabric, lift up the excess fabric and trim close to the stitching with a curved embroidery scissors, or as you would excess appliqué fabric.

*Designs that can be used for this technique:*

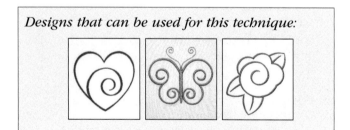

## Outline Appliqué

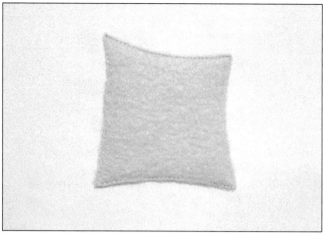

*Segment 2 of Appliqué Curved Square*

The simple outline of an appliqué design can be used with fabrics that do not ravel, such as fleece. Industry fleece expert, Nancy Cornwell, refers to this technique as Blunt Edge Appliqué. For more information on embroidery on fleece, refer to *Fleece Techniques* by Nancy Cornwell from the *Embroidery Machine Essentials: Companion Project Series*.

Fleece appliqué fabric can be stitched on woven as well as fleece base fabrics with the outline, blanket or satin stitch methods. The steps for this technique are illustrated with fleece on fleece.

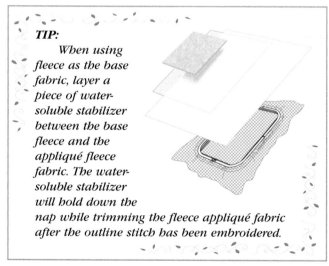

*TIP:*
*When using fleece as the base fabric, layer a piece of water-soluble stabilizer between the base fleece and the appliqué fleece fabric. The water-soluble stabilizer will hold down the nap while trimming the fleece appliqué fabric after the outline stitch has been embroidered.*

### Instructions:

1. Hoop a piece of mesh stabilizer. Spray the stabilizer with temporary adhesive and secure the base fleece to the hooped stabilizer. Place the hoop on the machine and stitch segment 1 (perimeter baste) of the Appliqué Curved Square.

2. Cut a piece of fleece appliqué fabric slightly larger than the perimeter baste. Place the piece on the base fleece while the hoop is on the machine and stitch segment 2 (outline).

3. Remove the hoop from the machine. Use a curved tip or appliqué scissors to trim close to the outline shape. Remove the fabric from the hoop, remove the perimeter basting stitches and trim away the excess stabilizer.

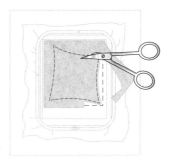

*Use a pinking shears to trim around the outline for a decorative touch.*

*Designs that can be used for this technique:*

## Reverse Appliqué

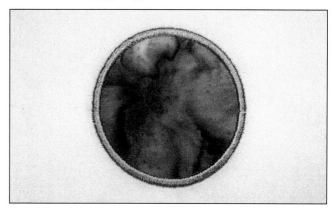

*Segment 5-7 of Circles (Satin)*

Most appliqué designs can be used with the Reverse Appliqué technique, too. This technique is the opposite of Appliqué and is the same as Sheer Cutwork (see page 18), where the inside of the motif is trimmed away to reveal another fabric.

### Instructions:

1. Hoop a layer of contrasting fabric between the base fabric and the stabilizer.

2. Place the hoop on the machine and stitch segment 1 (perimeter baste) and segment 6 (outline) of the Circles (Satin).

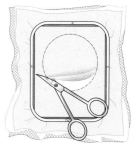

3. Remove the hoop from the machine; do not remove the fabric from the hoop. Trim away the fabric from the inside of the circle.

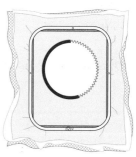

4. Place the hoop back on the machine and embroider segment 7 (zigzag) and 8 (satin stitch).

5. Remove the hoop from the machine and remove the fabric from the hoop. On the backside of the design, remove the excess stabilizer, remove the perimeter basting stitches, and trim away the excess appliqué fabric.

*Designs that can be used for this technique:*

## *Project Ideas*

### *Fall Fun*

This great lesson in appliqué is fun to create by using only segment 2 (outline) of any appliqué design on the accompanying CD-ROM and a non-raveling fabric. The appliqué leaves from the Appliqué Leaves & Stem combined with the Appliqué Curved Box outline is a simple to stitch border idea. Hoop the stabilizer, spray the stabilizer with a temporary adhesive, and secure the base fabric to the hooped stabilizer. This simple combination will make it easy to piece a continuous design down the side of jacket, cardigan or shirt with non-raveling appliqué fabric pieces.

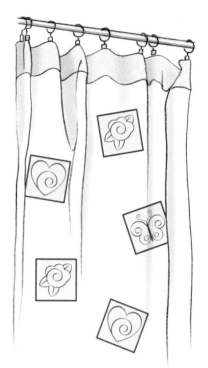

### *Sheer Delight*

Dress up a shower curtain by embroidering the Butterfly, Heart and Rose designs on two layers of organza and using a decorative stitch to stitch the embroidered fabric onto a shower curtain.

### *Appliqué Along*

The Curved Square combined with the Retro Circle make the perfect border print. Stitch the motifs down the front of a shirt, along the bottom edge of a jacket or across the edge of a pillowcase. Use appliqué fabric that coordinates with the other fabrics in the ensemble (clothing or home dec.)

# Chapter 3
# Quilting

*Elegant Star*

 uilting has long been a handwork tradition. The introduction of sewing machine quilting made the process quicker and now, embroidery machine quilting is by the far the easiest method. Even though hand quilting will continue to be a time-honored tradition, embroidery machine quilting is available for a quick-to-stitch technique.

Embroidery threads make the difference when it comes to quilting. Cotton threads are available in a variety of weights and are usually the best choice for the most traditional look on cotton fabrics. Be sure to experiment with variegated threads, too. Both variegated and shiny threads tend to stand out especially if the design has a multiple stitch pattern (double or triple bean stitches).

The most popular of quilt designs feature outline or running stitches. The simplistic nature of the stitches makes quilting type designs perfect for other embroidery techniques. Look for fun ideas using outline designs in Fleece Techniques by Nancy Cornwell, a part of the *Embroidery Machine Essentials: Companion Project Series*.

## *Quilting Methods*

There are two methods used for the quilting of a pieced quilt or wall hanging. Both methods resemble the look of traditional quilting and require the quilt to be completely finished without the binding.

## *Method 1*

The Butterfly, Rose (Outline) and Heart are easy-to-stitch quilting motifs perfect for this quilt project idea. Directions for making the quilt can be found on pages 78–79 in *Embroidery Machine Essentials*.

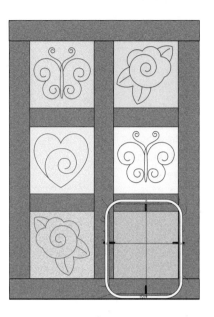

## Instructions:

1. Completely piece the quilt top. Add a very thin batting layer, cotton backing, and then pin the layers together.

2. Mark the placement of the design. Remove the pins that will interfere with the hooping of the area to be embroidered.

3. Loosen the hoop substantially. The quilt should be lightly hooped as the hoop is merely acting as a holder while the design is stitched. Gently, hoop the quilt.

4. During the embroidery process, hold the quilt up off the embroidery machine so the embroidery arm can move freely.

> ***NOTE:***
> *A stabilizer is not needed for this method, as the materials used to make the quilt are sturdy and will support the stitches during the embroidery process.*

## *Method 2*

## Instructions:

1. Hoop a layer of medium weight water-soluble stabilizer. Swipe the stabilizer with a damp sponge to make it sticky to the touch. Or, lightly spray the hooped stabilizer with a temporary adhesive.

2. Mark the placement of the design, secure the quilt to the stabilizer, place the hoop on the machine and embroider the design (including the perimeter baste). Be

sure to hold the quilt up off the embroidery machine as mentioned in Method 1.

3. After the embroidery process, remove the hoop from the machine and the perimeter basting stitches. Remove the excess stabilizer from the back of the quilt and dissolve any remaining pieces with a damp sponge on the back of the quilt.

*Designs that can be used for this technique:*

## Cotton Quilting

*Heart*

Outline designs are great for the "puffed-up" appearance when using individual batting pieces between the stabilizer and the base cotton fabric. For added "puff" in a quilt, use this method prior to sewing the quilt fabric sections together. This technique can be used in a variety of projects. Consider

"puffing up" any outline or quilt design on a T-shirt, sweatshirt, denim shirt and more.

**Instructions:**

1. Hoop a layer of mesh cut-away stabilizer.

2. Cut a piece of thin batting to fit inside the hoop.

3. Spray the batting with a fine mist of temporary adhesive and secure the base cotton fabric to the batting.

4. Place the hoop on the machine. Stitch segment 1 (perimeter baste) of the Heart design and then stitch segment 2 (outline).

5. Remove the hoop from the machine, the fabric from the hoop and the perimeter basting stitches.

6. To remove the excess batting and stabilizer, work with the fabric toward you and always in sight as you cut. Use a paper scissors to remove the excess batting and stabilizer on the backside. Do not use fabric scissors as the batting and stabilizer may dull the blades. An inexpensive paper scissors, used by children, works great.

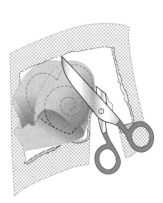

*Designs that can be used for this technique:*

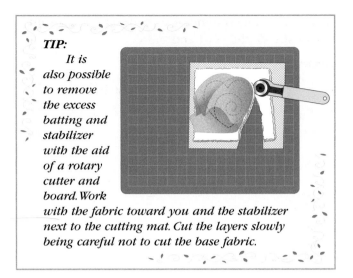

**TIP:**
*It is also possible to remove the excess batting and stabilizer with the aid of a rotary cutter and board. Work with the fabric toward you and the stabilizer next to the cutting mat. Cut the layers slowly being careful not to cut the base fabric.*

## Fleece Quilting

*Rose (Outline) on a high-loft fleece*

It is also possible to use the Cotton Quilting technique with fleece as the base fabric. Use a loftier batting if your machine has space under the presser foot. Without a water-soluble topping, the embroidery stitches will imbed into the fleece providing a dimensional effect. The stretch of the fleece, the loft of the batting and the color of the thread will all impact the "puffy" appearance of the design.

Use any outline or quilting design for this technique, especially if the design has large open areas. After the design is stitched, trim away the excess stabilizer and batting. Pull out away excess fleece poking out from behind the stabilizer, if necessary. A closer trim will result in a higher loft and less bulk on the backside of the garment.

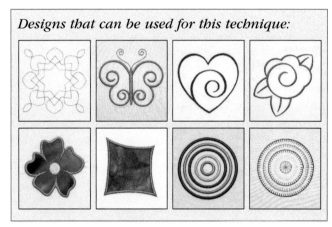

*Segment 2 of Butterfly on a low-loft fleece*

Nancy Cornwell, in *Fleece Techniques*, from the *Embroidery Machine Essentials: Companion Project Series,* refers to this technique as Trapunto with Batting. The loft and stretch of the fleece combined with the loft of the batting make this the perfect technique for fleece embroidery.

*Designs that can be used for this technique:*

15

## Project Ideas

### Wintry Wonder

Embellish a purchased or custom-made fleece jacket to show off your fleece quilting technique. The simplistic nature of the Rose (outline or satin) design combined with the accent colors of the collar, zipper and cuffs is a subtle accent for wintry fun.

### Home Dec Delight (Coordinating Sheets, Pillows and Sheers)

Coordinate an entire ensemble with the Butterfly, Heart and Rose embroidery designs. From dressing up a top sheet to using machine stitches with the butterflies to show dimension, these three designs were created for swirls of fun. Embroider directly on sheer curtains and use long double sewing machine stitches to show the flight of the butterfly design.

# Chapter 4
# Cutwork

utwork is the technique where fabric within the center of a design is cut out and the cut edges are finished with Satin Stitches. There are a variety of methods for Cutwork each being a bit time consuming, but well worth the effort.

Traditional Cutwork results in planned holes in the fabric, Sheer Cutwork results in a sheer backing to protect the integrity of the fabric, and Layered Cutwork results in a multiple sheer "windowpane" effect in the fabric. All methods are best stitched with a woven fabric as the base material. For more information about Cutwork, refer to page 56 in *Embroidery Machine Essentials*.

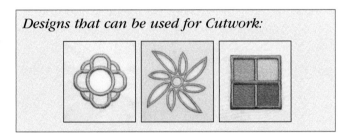

*Designs that can be used for Cutwork:*

## Traditional Cutwork

*Cutwork Flower*

This technique requires a bit of precision while cutting the fabric as to not disturb delicate tear-away stabilizer beneath and prevent distortion of the fabric.

**Instructions:**

1. Hoop a layer of light tear-away stabilizer with the base woven fabric. Place the hoop on the machine. Stitch segment 1 (perimeter baste) of the Cutwork Flower and then segment 2 (double outline).

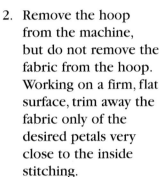

2. Remove the hoop from the machine, but do not remove the fabric from the hoop. Working on a firm, flat surface, trim away the fabric only of the desired petals very close to the inside stitching.

3. Return the hoop to the machine and finish stitching the design. When the design is complete, remove the hoop from the machine and the perimeter basting stitches. Remove the fabric from the hoop and remove the stabilizer from within the petals and around the outer edge. The stabilizer should tear-away easily. Any remaining stabilizer should wash away during the first laundry treatment.

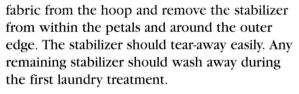

## *Sheer Cutwork*

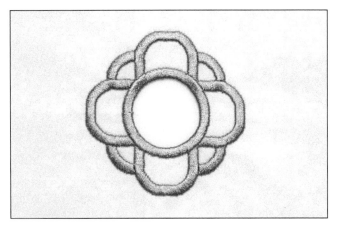

*Cutwork Celtic*

A layer of a sheer fabric behind the base fabric can add stability to the project after the cutwork process. Use a sheer "skin color" layer of organza for invisible "holes" in the fabric.

### Instructions:

1. Hoop a layer of sheer organza or organdy between the base woven fabric and the light tear-away stabilizer. Place the hoop on the machine. Stitch segment 1 (perimeter baste) and segment 2 (double outline) of the Cutwork Celtic design.

2. Remove the hoop from the machine, but do not remove the fabric from the hoop. Working on a firm, flat surface, trim away the fabric of the desired sections very close to the inside stitching.

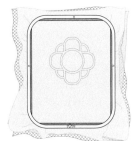

3. Return the hoop to the machine and finish stitching the design. When the design is complete, remove the hoop from the machine, the fabric from the hoop and the perimeter basting stitches. On the backside of the design, tear away the stabilizer and trim the sheer fabric close to the outside stitching.

## *Layered Cutwork*

*Cutwork Squares*

Use the Cutwork Squares design to experiment with multiple colors of organza to achieve the "windowpane" effect. This technique requires a tightly woven base fabric that can withstand hooping on its own.

### Instructions:

1. Hoop the base fabric without a stabilizer. Place the hoop on the machine and slide four sheer layers of organza or organdy under the hoop.

2. Stitch segment 1 (perimeter baste) and segment 2 (double outline) to secure the layers together. Remove the hoop from the machine.

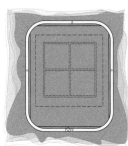

3. Remove the perimeter basting stitches. On the backside of the hoop, trim away all the excess sheer layers on the outside edge of the stitching.

Back

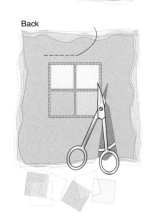

4. From the front and the back of the design, trim away the layers in each box to expose a different color in each square.

5. Return the hoop to the machine and slide a layer of lightweight tear-away stabilizer under the hoop. Stitch the remainder of the design.

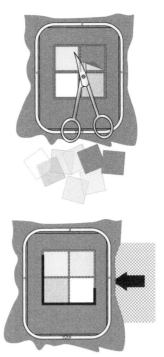

- - - - - - - - - - - - - - - - - - - - - - - - - - - - - - - - - - - - - - - - - - - - - - - - - - - - - - - -

## *Project Ideas*

### *Cutwork T-shirt*

Cutwork on knit fabric? With a backing of organdy to hold the shape. Use the Sheer Cutwork method found on page 18 with colorful pieces of sheer organza.

### *Celtic Shirt*

Snap up a purchased or custom-made denim shirt with the Cutwork Celtic design embroidered on organza or organdy. Remove the buttons from the shirt and replace the closure with snaps. Follow the Dimensional (Satin Stitch) instructions found on page 20 to embroider the design. Trim the excess organdy or organza and use a hot knife to melt the excess fabric close to the stitching.

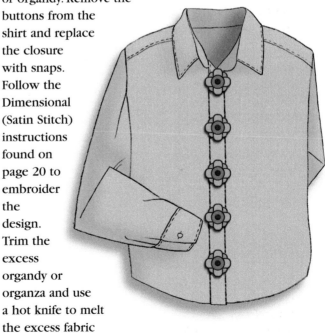

# Chapter 5
## Artful Expressions

This chapter will help stretch your imagination by showing how to embroider designs in a unique way for creative surface texture. From texturizing fleece to rubberstamping, this is where the adventure in creativity begins!

## *Dimensional*

*Appliqué Flower*

Surface embellishment can achieve new heights with Dimensional Embroidery. Any Satin Stitch design has the potential to become dimensional — raised off the surface of the base fabric. Most satin stitch finish designs offer the best potential for this technique. For more information about Dimensional Embroidery, refer to page 61 in *Embroidery Machine Essentials*.

## *Satin Stitch*

*Cutwork Celtic*

The Cutwork Celtic is a great design to practice your Dimensional embroidery skills. For a little color variety, use two layers of contrasting organza.

For a firmer dimensional application, back the layers of organza with a sheer cream color heavy organdy.

**Instructions:**

1. Hoop two layers of nylon organza perpendicular to each other. Embroider the entire Cutwork Celtic design with synthetic thread.

2. Remove the hoop from the machine and remove the fabric from the hoop. Trim away the excess fabric close to the satin stitch edge finish.

3. Use a hot knife or wood-burning tool to swiftly melt away the fabric edges close to the stitching.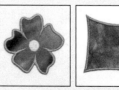

*TIP:*
> It is best to practice using the hot knife or wood-burning tool on scrap pieces of organza or organdy fabric before attempting this technique on the actual project. Quick swift movements are best as to prevent burning of the fabric and thread.

*Designs that can be used for this technique:*

## *Cut Edge*

*Appliqué Flower*

Appliqué designs can make perfect fleece dimensional motifs. Secure the fleece dimensional motif to the base fabric using the center stitching of a design, a long-prong snap or a button.

### Instructions:

1. Hoop a layer of fleece in the smallest hoop that will accommodate the design. Place the hoop on the machine and stitch segment 2 (flower outline) of the Appliqué Flower.

2. Remove the hoop from the machine and remove the fabric from the hoop. Trim away the excess fabric using the outline as the cutting guide.

3. Secure the dimensional motif to the fabric using a long-prong snap or the center of the flower (segment 5 and 6).

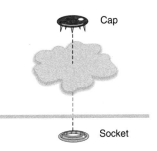

Cap

Socket

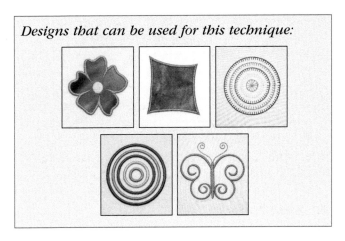

*Designs that can be used for this technique:*

## *Texturing Fleece*

*Segment 2 of the Retro Circle, Retro Square and Retro Triangle*

The texturing of fleece can be accomplished in a variety of ways. The three Retro designs, with their uniform underlay stitches, can compress the fleece resulting in an "imprint" on fleece. This "imprint" can be stitched with a color coordinating high sheen thread for subtle results or with a bright contrasting thread for more dramatic results. The loft of the fleece will determine the "imprint" depth.

For more fleece texture fun, refer to Nancy Cornwell's *Fleece Techniques* book, part of the *Embroidery Machine Essentials: Companion Project Series.*

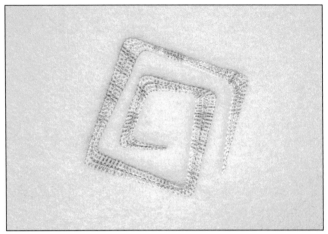

*Segment 2 of the Retro Square on a low-loft fleece without a water-soluble topping.*

## Instructions:

1. Hoop a layer of light-weight water-soluble stabilizer. Spray the hooped stabilizer with temporary adhesive. Mark the fabric and secure the fleece to the stabilizer.

2. If desired, add a water-soluble topping.

3. Place the hoop on the machine. Stitch segment 1 (perimeter baste) and segment 2 of the Retro Circle.

4. Remove the hoop from the machine and the fabric from the hoop. Remove the perimeter basting stitches and tear-away the excess stabilizer from the back of the fabric.

*Optional water-soluble topping*

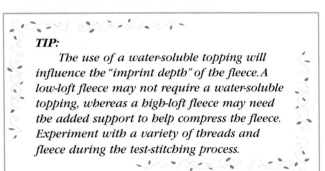

> **TIP:**
> The use of a water-soluble topping will influence the "imprint depth" of the fleece. A low-loft fleece may not require a water-soluble topping, whereas a high-loft fleece may need the added support to help compress the fleece. Experiment with a variety of threads and fleece during the test-stitching process.

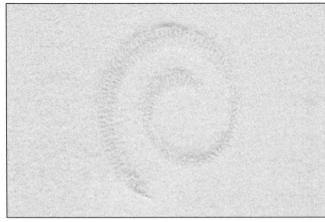

*Segment 2 of the Retro Circle on a high-loft fleece without a water-soluble topping*

The photo above shows the stitches imbedded into the nap of the fabric without the use of a water-soluble topping. The photo below shows that a water-soluble topping was used to tame the nap during the embroidery process. Both are fine for texturizing, it all depends on the look you desire.

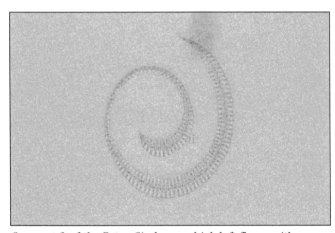

*Segment 2 of the Retro Circle on a high-loft fleece with a water-soluble topping*

*Designs that can be used for this technique:*

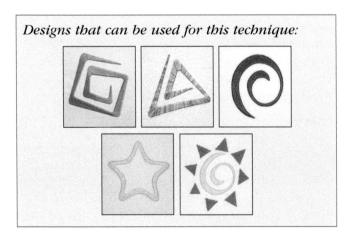

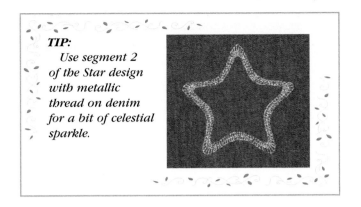

## Fringing

*Fringed Flowers*

Designs that contain overly long stitches for fringing are planned at the digitizing level. The Fringed Flowers design on the CD-ROM was digitized specifically for the Fringing technique. The long stitches are held down by short compact stitches and the bobbin threads are snipped to allow the long stitches to be pulled to the surface.

The embroidery machine tension will determine the amount of bobbin thread that is exposed on the back of the design. The more bobbin thread exposed, the smaller the fringing. For best results, lower the machine tension, use a rayon or cotton thread for the long stitches and a burst of steam from an iron to remove the kink in the thread after the embroidery process.

### Instructions:

1. Hoop the fabric with the appropriate stabilizer. Place the hoop on the machine and stitch segment 1 (perimeter baste) of the Fringed Flowers and then the remainder of the design. Remove the hoop from the machine; do not remove the fabric from the hoop.

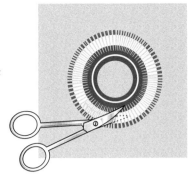

2. On the back of the hooped fabric, use a curved embroidery scissors to cut the thread closest to the center circle stitching. Cut the threads within 1/8" from the stitching being careful not to cut the top threads that have been pulled to the back by the bobbin threads.

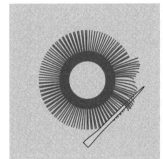

3. Remove the bobbin thread. It should pull away with ease.

4. On the front of the design, gently pull up on the long stitches with your fingers, an awl or a thin crochet hook until all the threads are on top of the fabric.

### Optional Method:

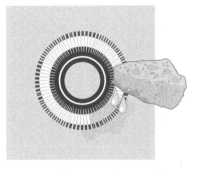

An alternative method is to use a water-soluble thread in the bobbin instead of standard bobbin thread.

Hand wind a bobbin with water-soluble thread and use it to stitch segments 2, 4 and 6. Use a wet sponge to remove the thread after the embroidery process.

Mark the bobbin to indicate that the bobbin is special and keep the bobbin in a small zip locked bag to prevent the thread from drying out. Be sure to change back to standard sewing thread when stitching segments 3, 5 and 7 or else the design will completely disappear!

## Double Needle

*Segment 2 of the Heart*

If one needle can stitch embroidery designs, why can't two? For best results use designs that contain outline segments such as quilting, appliqué or running stitches. A variety of effects can be achieved depending on the spacing between the needles. On fleece, use a wide double needle (3.0) and on cotton fabrics use a narrow double needle (2.0). Be sure to check with the dealer that holds your warranty for verification that this technique can be used on your machine.

Be sure to test-stitch designs with a single needle before attempting a double needle. Then, be sure to test-stitch the design with a double needle to verify compatibility.

*Segment 2 of the Heart (backside)*

When test-stitching designs with double needles, check out the backside of the fabric. Sometimes the backside looks better than the front! For more on double needle techniques on fleece, check out *Fleece Techniques* by Nancy Cornwell, a part of the *Embroidery Machine Essentials: Companion Project Series*.

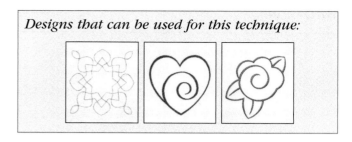

*Designs that can be used for this technique:*

## Arts & Crafts

*Retro designs and coordinating rubberstamps*

Adding yet another dimension to embroidery can yield exciting results. Try mixing embroidery with paints, stencils and rubberstamps. The crossing over between sewing and embroidery, and from embroidery to arts and crafts is called "mixed media."

When mixing different forms of media with embroidery, take into consideration the end result. For example, use a synthetic embroidery thread with watercolor paints as to not affect the thread color. Or, consider using a white cotton embroidery thread purposefully so that the thread color will change with the addition of paint.

Always, pre-wash fabrics without a softener before adding paint to the mix. Be sure to follow the manufacturer's instructions for heat-setting the paint to the fabric. Keep in mind the type of thread used for the paint heat-setting process and use a press cloth when coming in contact with the thread.

A variety of fabrics can be used for these techniques. From sweatshirt fabric to canvas, 100% cotton will absorb and retain the paint best. Test-stitch, experiment with paint and launder for best results.

## Watercolor

*Rose (Outline) painted with watercolor paint*

Redwork, blackwork, bluework, quilting and outline designs make the best watercolor templates. Simply embroider and paint!

Standard watercolor paints work best for this technique. Be sure to protect clothing and the work surface during the painting process. Use a bowl of water for rinsing the paintbrush, plenty of paper towel to wipe excess water from the brush and extra fabric to experiment using this technique.

### Instructions:

1. Hoop the base fabric with the appropriate stabilizer. Place the hoop on the machine and stitch segment 2 of the Elegant Star. Remove the hoop from the machine, the fabric from the hoop and the stabilizer from the fabric. Press the design on the fabric wrong side using a press cloth.

2. Prepare of bowl of water for rinsing the brush and open up the watercolor container.

3. Dip the brush in water, dab the brush onto a piece of paper towel and then onto the first color in the watercolor container. Dab the brush onto the paper towel again to determine if the consistency of the paint is correct. Experiment with techniques to determine the appropriate ratio of paint and water.

4. Paint one color at a time. Pause between colors to heat-set and dry the paint before moving onto the next color so as not to mix the colors on the fabric. Start with the lightest colors and end with the darkest color. Change the water in the bowl frequently.

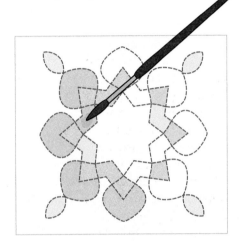

*Designs that can be used for this technique:*

## Rubberstamps

*Retro designs mixed with rubberstamps*

The addition of rubberstamps and textile paint to embroidery is a fun way to add dimension to finished projects. To get you started, Dana Botranger from Purrfection (see Resources on page 47) created see-through rubberstamps to coordinate with the Retro Circle, Retro Square and Retro Triangle. These rubberstamps are clear so you can see through to the fabric for precision placement.

Use rubberstamps to add subtle color to fabric before the embroidery process. Or, better yet, embellish solid color white or cream cotton fabric to coordinate with the embroidered motifs.

Use paints made specifically for fabric. Follow the manufacturer's instructions to heat-set the paint to the fabric. For best results, use a paint pallet for mixing paint, a make-up sponge for applying paint (or a brayer), and paper towel for the dabbing of excess paint before stamping the fabric. Be sure to clean rubberstamps when changing paint colors and after the completion of a project.

Consider purchasing a color wheel for the mixing of colors. A color wheel will help with not only the mixing of colors but also coordinating embroidery thread colors to paints or other embroidery thread colors.

## Instructions:

1. Use a paint pallet to place droplets of paint colors. Be sure to add white and black for lightening or darkening colors. Use a plastic spoon to mix colors before dipping the sponge into mixed colors.

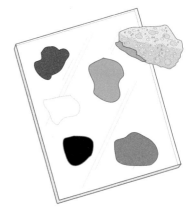

2. Use a make-up sponge or brayer to spread paint on to the rubberstamp image as shown.

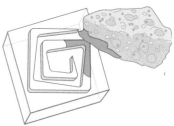

3. Place a piece of cardboard covered with wax paper under the fabric to provide a firm surface and to prevent the paint from bleeding through to another layer of fabric (i.e., purchased sweatshirt or T-shirt). Press the painted rubberstamp image evenly onto the fabric. Lift the rubberstamp up evenly off the fabric. Repeat as desired.

4. Allow the paint to thoroughly cure before heat setting and adding embroidery to the fabric.

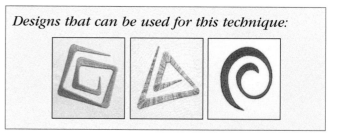

*Designs that can be used for this technique:*

## *Project Ideas*

### *Simple Tee & Shorts*

For summer, and kids of all ages, add a touch of embroidery at the hem of shorts or the bottom edge of a T-shirt using one of the Retro designs. The embroidery accent is subtle, yet fashionable. When using ready-made clothing, be sure to turn the item inside out to embroider and do not hoop the fabric. Rather, hoop the stabilizer and spray the stabilizer with temporary adhesive. Secure the fabric to the stabilizer and use segment 1 (perimeter baste) to hold the layers together.

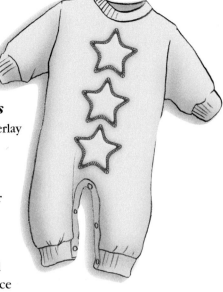

### *Fleece Jammies*

Segment 2 (underlay stitches) of the Star makes the perfect accent on fleece pajamas. Use a color the same as or contrasting to the base fabric. Use a water-soluble topping and the Texturizing Fleece instructions found on page 21. Hoop a layer of water-soluble stabilizer and spray it with a temporary adhesive. Then, turn the jammies inside out, secure the outfit to the stabilizer and embroider the design through the opening in the neck or legs.

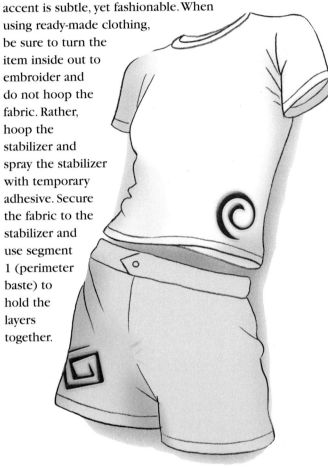

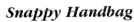

### *Snappy Handbag*

The Dimensional technique using the Cutwork Celtic is perfect for placement on both sides of a fashion handbag. Use thread colors that coordinate with the purse and organza or organdy as the base material. Secure a reversible prong style snap through the center of the design and the handbag for the perfect embroidered closure.

## Shapely Slipcover

A slipcover and the retro shapes of the Triangle, Circle and Square are perfect together. Fit the slipcover to your couch and mark the placement of the designs. The weight of the slipcover could overpower the embroidery machine, so be sure to hold the cover up off the bed of the machine and the hoop during the embroidery process. Add pillow accents using the same designs. Consider making your own embellished fabric for the pillow by rubber-stamping the pillow with the same or embroider the motifs for a creative accent.

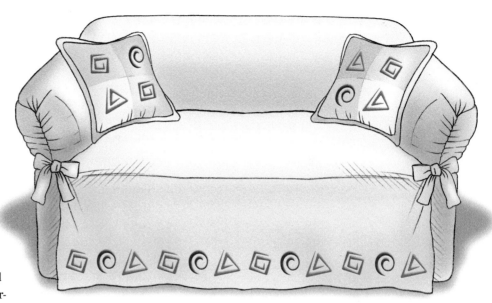

## Fringy Handbag

Combine the Fringed Flowers with the sprigs of the Flower Spray to accentuate this handbag. Use a ready-made bag or custom-make one, if desired. To embroider deep inside a handbag, open up the side seam to accommodate the reach of the embroidery hoop. Eliminate the flowers from the Flower Spray and save each leaf sprig in a separate file. Combine and straighten the designs within customizing software.

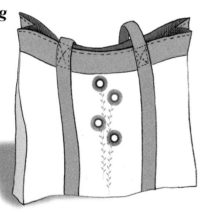

## Retro Pillows

What teen wouldn't love these retro-style pillow made from brightly colored fleece and embroidered with the Retro Circle. Make the flower shape pillow similar to a box-style pillow and stuff the pillow shape with fiberfill.

# Chapter 6
# Combining and Editing Designs

*Appliqué Flower, Appliqué Leaves & Stem, and Sun*

here are two ways to combine and edit embroidery designs — on the touch screen of an embroidery machine, or with embroidery software on a computer. The designs on the CD-ROM have segments that can be combined, rotated, enlarged, reduced, edited, colorized and more. Utilizing embroidery software is the preferred method for combining designs and editing stitches.

**NOTE:**

*In order to combine or edit the designs included with this book, you must have a hoop for your embroidery machine larger than 4" x 4". The designs can be customized for use in a 5" x 7" or larger hoop. In addition, the software chosen to combine or edit designs must have the appropriate size hoop measurements for your embroidery equipment.*

Be sure to check with your embroidery machine dealer or the Web site of your embroidery machine manufacturer (see Resources page 47) to obtain the latest updates for your embroidery machine and compatible software. If you need assistance determining the capabilities of your embroidery equipment, consult the dealer that holds the warranty for your machine. Some dealers often hold monthly Embroidery Club gatherings, provide personal consultations (sometimes for a fee), or have the latest tutorials from independent educators on utilizing embroidery machines and software should you need help.

Use the design templates (printed from the PDF files on the CD-ROM) to layout a plan for design customization. Then, use the touch screen on your embroidery machine or your embroidery software to alter the designs according your plan. Refer to pages 33-35 for some ideas to combine the designs. Refer to page 45 in *Embroidery Machine Essentials* on how to make and use design templates.

## Using an Embroidery Machine

In order to use an embroidery machine to manipulate designs, the on-board screen must be large enough to show the design and hoop size details, open multiple designs on the touch screen, and have enough memory to save the new customized design.  If your embroidery machine cannot perform these tasks, then embroidery software will offer the greatest opportunity for combining designs.

For more accurate design placement, turn the background grid feature "ON", if available for your embroidery machine. This grid feature is similar to graph paper with interconnecting lines in equal increments and will help with design alignment. The grid is used only for alignment and will not embroider onto projects.

Next, make sure the appropriate hoop size appears on the screen. To combine the designs featured in this book, it will be necessary to use a hoop larger than a standard 4" x 4" size. By using the screen grid and the outline of the hoop, you will be more successful with the opening and placement of designs.

When using the embroidery machine to manipulate designs, keep in mind that the entire design will be transferred to the embroidery machine. If you want to combine and stitch only a couple segments of a design, it may be necessary to move the hoop between segments to align designs. Some machines have the ability to move the hoop once the embroidery process begins, while others require the design be reloaded and the embroidery started at the appropriate segment. Embroidery machines, that have editing capabilities directly on the embroidery machine, will make the combining of segments easier.

1.  Transfer the desired embroidery design(s) to the embroidery machine through a disk, CD-ROM, cable, read/writer box, or PC card.

2.  Use the owner's manual to determine how to combine, rotate, size, save and stitch customized designs on your embroidery machine. Be sure to start the customizing process on the appropriate screen. And, be sure that the grid and hoop are visible, if this feature is available on your embroidery machine.

3.  Open the first design onto the touch screen. Move and rotate the design using the direction arrows or finger pressure on the screen to position the image on the grid.

4.  Open the next design and repeat the process of moving and rotating the design into the desired location. Repeat, if necessary.

5.  If you want to reposition the first design, it will be necessary to touch or select the desired design again. A box around the design usually indicates the active design that can be adjusted.

6.  Some machines may load designs directly in the center of the hoop each time a design appears on the screen. This could cause some confusion.

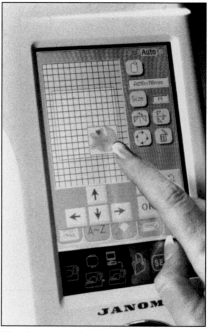

*Touch screen of a Janome embroidery machine.*

Always look for the design that is highlighted or boxed to know which design can be moved and determine if there are any hidden designs behind a highlighted box.

7.  Once you've finished with the customization, save the design on the embroidery machine, a disk, or a PC card before stitching the design. Some machines allow the saving or transferring of a customized design back to a computer through a cable, disk, CD-ROM, card or other technology. Should a power glitch cause the machine to power down before saving the customized design, your design may be lost. It is always a good idea to save the design before beginning the embroidery process.

8.  Once the design is saved, start the embroidery process. If the designs used for customization are whole, then it will be very important to pay attention to the design segments being stitched. It may be necessary to fast-forward through certain designs to achieve the technique desired for the project.

## Using Embroidery Software

By far, the easiest and fastest way to customize or manipulate designs is with a computer and embroidery software. Each design segment is digitized with a stop to make the design parts easy to extract using embroidery software. There are over 65 stitch variations hidden amongst the 20 designs. Each one can be extracted and saved to a new file for use in customizing unique designs.

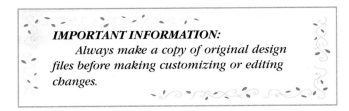

**IMPORTANT INFORMATION:**
*Always make a copy of original design files before making customizing or editing changes.*

## Combining Designs

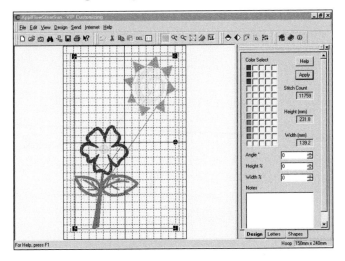

Customizing software can be used to combine, rotate, size and move designs to avoid manual placement. The process for combining designs on the touch screen of the embroidery machine is very similar to the method on a computer. The main difference is speed. Extracting the design segments in a stitch editing software will further speed the customization process and eliminate the need to forward through designs to find segments on the embroidery machine for techniques. The computer will do the work for you.

For more accurate design placement, turn "ON" the background grid. To combine designs featured in this book, it will be necessary to use a hoop

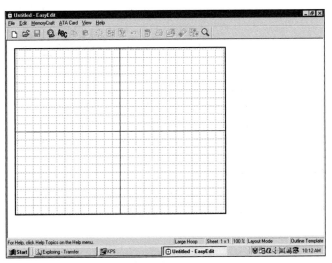

*Background grid turned "ON."*

larger than a standard 4" x 4" in order to customize a series of designs together. Be sure the appropriate hoop size appears on the screen. By using the screen grid and the outline of the hoop, you will be more successful when customizing unique designs.

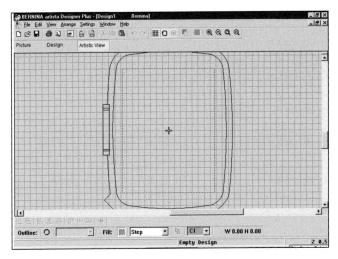

1. Start the customizing process with a new file in the customizing software.

2. Open the first design. Move and rotate the design using the mouse or keyboard arrows to position the image in place.

3. Open the next design and repeat the process of moving and rotating the design into the desired location. Repeat, if necessary.

4. If you want to reposition any one of the designs, it will be necessary to use the mouse to highlight the desired design again for the software to recognize the design that needs to be moved.

5. Some software may load designs directly in the center of the hoop. Use the mouse to move the designs away from the center and into position. Always look for the design that is highlighted or boxed to know which one can be moved.

6. Once you've finished with the customization, it may be necessary to group the designs so that the embroidery machine understands to stitch the individual designs as one complete design.

7. Save the design and close the file. Transfer the design to your embroidery machine to test-stitch the "new" design.

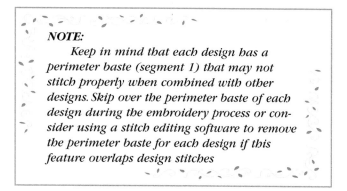

> **NOTE:**
> *Keep in mind that each design has a perimeter baste (segment 1) that may not stitch properly when combined with other designs. Skip over the perimeter baste of each design during the embroidery process or consider using a stitch editing software to remove the perimeter baste for each design if this feature overlaps design stitches*

## Editing Stitches

*Stitch editing Heart and Flower Spray combination*

A stitch editor is used to manipulate stitches by moving and deleting design segments, or by adding one stitch at a time. Each design segment can be extracted from the original design and saved to a separate file for combining with other designs.

1. Load a design into a stitch editing software.

2. Save the design as a new file name using the "save as" function.

3. It may be necessary to highlight the design first before editing the design. Do so by using the computer mouse to rope, click or box in the entire design area.

4. Forward through the design by color. At each change in color, it is possible to delete, extract or move the segment. When forwarding through the colors, delete the unnecessary segments and keep the segments needed to embroider the design as intended.

5. Resave the design and close the file.

6. Transfer the design to your embroidery machine to test-stitch the "new" design.

## Design Extraction

*Rose (Outline)*          *Rose (Satin)*

For example purposes, the Rose (Outline) and Rose (Satin) designs are provided on the accompanying CD-ROM in 2 separate files. The other 18 designs were digitized in layers with stops denoting the change in a segment.

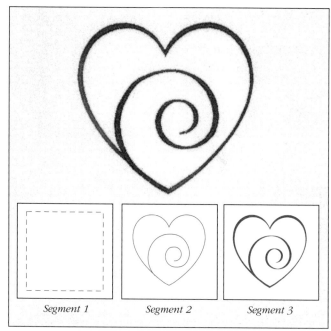

*Segment 1*     *Segment 2*     *Segment 3*

*Heart and stitch segments*

The Heart design has the same segments (outline and satin) as the two Rose files. The Rose designs are already split into two files whereas the Heart design is still one file. It is very easy to separate the Heart design into two files by using a stitch editing software.

1. Load the Heart design into a stitch editing software.

2. Resave the Heart design into two files similar to the Rose designs — one, "save as" Heart Outline and two, "save as" Heart Satin.

> **NOTE:**
> *If your software requires 8 character file names, be sure to save the files accurately with the appropriate format for your embroidery machine.*

3. To start the editing process, open the Heart Outline file. It may be necessary to highlight the design first before editing the design. Do so by using the computer mouse to rope, click or box in the entire design area.

4. Forward through the design by color. At each change in color (segment stop), it is possible to delete, extract or move the segment. Stop at segment 3 (satin stitches). Delete this segment of the design following the software instructions.

5. Resave the design and close the file.

6. Open the Heart Satin file. Forward through the design and stop at segment 2 (outline). Delete this segment of the design.

7. Resave the design and close the file.

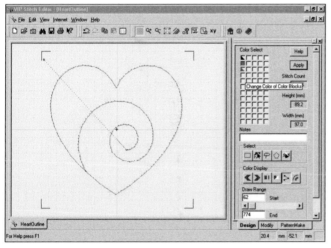

*Heart (Outline) new file*

8. Transfer the designs to your embroidery machine to test-stitch the "new" designs.

There are other uses for editing software, such as enlarging or reducing a design, determining the stitch count and size of design segments, and more. Editing and combining designs can be a fun way to expand your embroidery design collection.

## Design Combinations

Here are some ideas for combining designs. Use your embroidery machine or software to combine the designs. Be sure to use the Appendix: Design Details starting on page 43 as your guide.

### *Retro Triangle* (Rotated two ways)

### *Sun and Flower Spray*

The Sun and mini flowers from the Flower Spray combined with machine stitches.

## Appliqué Flower and Flower Spray

## Retro Circles

## Flower Spray *(Mirror imaged)*

## Circles *(Satin)*

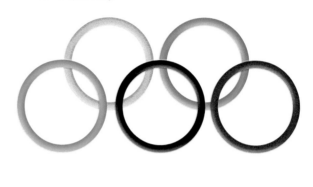

## Fringed Flowers and Flower Spray

## Retro Circle, Sun, and Appliqué Curved Square

## Leaves from the Appliqué Leaves & Stem and Appliqué Curved Square

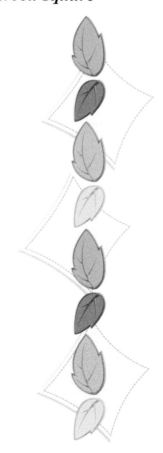

**Stem and Leaves** *(Used to create a bouquet of "Flowers")*
Appliqué Flower, Circles (Satin), Cutwork Celtic, Heart, Sun and Cutwork Flower

**Retro Circle and Sun**

**Butterflies** *(With hand stitches)*          **Stars**

## Project Ideas

### Triangle Twist

Here's a great exercise for customizing designs in software or on the touch screen of your embroidery machine. Load or open the Retro Triangle design into your customizing software or on the embroidery machine. Rotate the triangle into position. Continue to load or open the Retro Triangle until all the designs have been placed. Be sure the hoop size is appropriate to accommodate the size of the new design. If only half the design will fit in the hoop, then customize only one-half of the design. Stitch the design onto the sweatshirt. Then, rehoop and mirror image the design to stitch the other side of the design to make the complete triangle circle.

### Summer Sunshine

Stitch only segment 5 (flowers) of the Flower Spray in three hooping across the bottom front of a shirt. Add a ray of sunshine with the Sun design and long double running sewing machine stitches as the stems. When stitching the stems, pin a piece of lightweight tear-away or tissue paper behind the fabric during the sewing machine stitching. For best results turn the shirt inside out and sew from the bottom edge to the flowers.

### Spring Fling

The sprigs of the Flower Spray make a great tonal accent on this springtime dress. Use a stitch editor to remove the segment 5 (flowers) from the design. Then, one at a time, isolate each sprig and save the individual sprigs in separate files (i.e., small sprig, medium spring, and large sprig). Randomly place the sprigs onto the bottom of a dress to make an all-over embroidered fabric. For more information on creating an all-over embroidered fabric, refer to page 66 in *Embroidery Machine Essentials*.

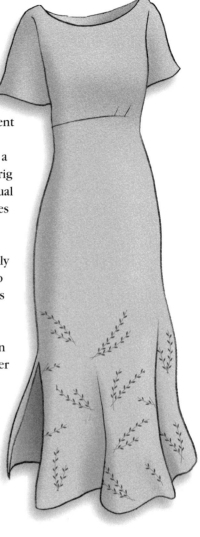

### Appliqué Flower Spray

Combine both the Appliqué Flower and the Flower Spray for a fun accent on a purchased or custom-made tank top. The combination of these two designs is perfect across the upper chest, the back yoke of a shirt, or a pillowcase header.

# Chapter 7
# Gallery of Project Ideas

Here are some quick-to-stitch project ideas to help utilize the embroidery techniques found within the pages of this book. Keep in mind that the projects can be embroidered with any design and that there is always more than one way to embroider a design. Let your personal preference be your guide.

The colors that appear on the screen of your embroidery machine are only representative of a color or segment change. Depending on your embroidery machine, the colors may be off. Use any thread color you desire for the designs depending on the base color of the project. Be sure to refer to the Appendix: Design Details starting on page 43 for segment stitching information. In most cases, you'll be fast-forwarding through the designs to find the segment for a particular technique. The Design Details will help you match up the segment with the part of the design you wish to stitch.

As noted in Chapter 1, each design features a perimeter basting stitch, which is optional depending on the project or fabrics to be embroidered. In most instances, the perimeter baste is utilized to hold the fabric and stabilizer layers together during the embroidery process.

Depending on the project, some added sewing might be required. When using a home embroidery and sewing machine, follow your owner's manual instructions to switch from embroidery to a sewing mode to stitch up the projects.

Use the following basic embroidery supplies for each project unless otherwise noted:

### Basic Embroidery Supplies:
- Design appropriate for the project
- Fabric or purchased item appropriate for the technique
- Stabilizer appropriate for the fabric or purchased item
- Temporary marking pen/pencil
- Embroidery machine needle – size appropriate for the project and thread
- Decorative embroidery thread
- Bobbin thread
- Hoop – smallest size for the design
- Sharp, curved, and straight blade scissors
- Spray adhesive

### Basic Sewing Supplies:
- Sewing thread to match the fabric
- Standard sewing machine needles: Ballpoint for knits; Sharps for wovens
- Iron and ironing board
- Press cloth
- Standard straight stitch sewing presser foot
- Serger (optional)

### Denim Delight

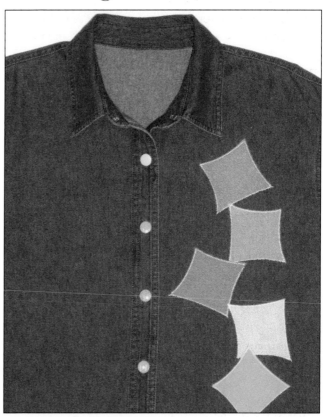

A denim shirt makes the perfect canvas for a variety of techniques. Embroider any one of the design combinations featured on pages 33-35 to embellish the fabric.

Use the Stitch & Trim Appliqué technique found on page 8 to appliqué the colorful patches onto the shirt. With a silvery gray color thread, stitch segment 2 (outline), trim the excess fabric and 3 (zigzag) of the Appliqué Flower. Remove the buttons and replace the closures with colorful snap fasteners that coordinate with the appliqué fabrics. For more information on Appliqué techniques, see Chapter 2.

*Designs that can be used for this project:*

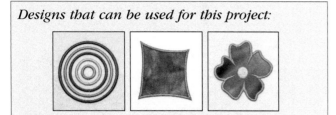

## Fleece Finesse

One of the easiest forms of texturing high-loft fleece is with the underlay stitches of a masterfully digitized design. Use the Texturing Fleece technique found on page 21 to hold down the nap of the fabric while stitching an impression of the design using the underlay stitches of the Retro Triangle and Retro Square.

Hoop a layer of lightweight water-soluble stabilizer and spray the stabilizer with a temporary adhesive. Secure the fleece to the stabilizer, add another layer of lightweight water-soluble stabilizer

as a topping, and stitch segment 1 (perimeter baste) of either the Retro Square or Retro Triangle. Then, stitch segment 2 (underlay stitches). Rehoop as desired.

*Designs that can be used for this technique:*

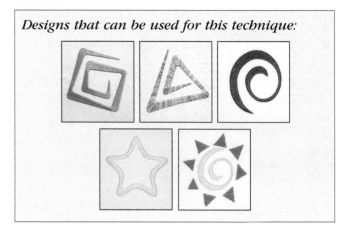

## All Tied Up!

Here's a no-sew pillow that's fun to embroider and quick to tie up. Use the Outline Appliqué technique found on page 10 and the Circles (Blanket) to embellish the fleece fabric.

The pillow is stuffed with a pillow form – a size of your choice. Add 8" to the size of your pillow form. Cut two pieces of coordinating fleece fabric this measurement – perpendicular to each other. With wrong sides of the cut fleece fabrics together, cut 1" fringes 4" long on all four sides (4" corner squares will be trimmed away in the process).

Hoop a layer of lightweight water-soluble stabilizer and spray the stabilizer with a temporary adhesive. Secure the top layer of the pillow fleece to the stabilizer, add another layer of lightweight water-soluble stabilizer as a topping, and stitch segment 4, 6 or 8 (outline) of the Circles (Blanket). Rehoop and randomly stitch circles as desired.

After the embroidery process, place the top layer of the pillow fleece to the bottom layer with wrong sides together. Tie the fringes together in knots. Leave one complete edge open for insertion of the pillow form. Insert the pillow form and tie the remaining edge.

## Sweet Sleep

The artful technique of combining rubberstamps with embroidery is sure to make this easy-to-stitch project one of your favorites. Use the pillowcase embroidery and construction information found on page 77 of *Embroidery Machine Essentials* to complete the project. The see-through rubber stamps from Purrfection (see Resources on page 47), that coordinate with the Retro Circle, Retro Triangle and Retro Square, are perfect for stamping onto the case fabric. Be sure to use fabric paint that is soft to the touch when dry for the ultimate in sleep comfort next to the skin. The embroidery is completed on the header before the construction of the pillowcase.

Use the rubberstamps to make your own fabric to coordinate with the embroidery designs for a variety of projects from the base fabric of a blanket to clothing. There are unlimited uses for just the stamps, too. Rubberstamp a lamp, bed sheets, pajamas, shower curtain, window treatments and more.

*Designs that can be used for this technique:*

## Handy Handbag Duo

These handy accessories are made from old jeans. Use a favorite tote bag and zippered purse pattern for the completion of this great ensemble. While any embroidery design can be used for this project, the Sun from the accompanying CD-ROM makes a cheery choice.

Closely cut away a back pocket from an old pair of jeans. Mark the center of the pocket, hoop a cut-away stabilizer, spray the stabilizer with a temporary adhesive, and secure the pocket into position on the stabilizer. Embroider the Sun design using a water-soluble stabilizer on top to prevent the stitches from imbedding into the denim. After the embroidery process, cut out the tote bag using the pattern and coordinating denim. Or, for a color coordinating appearance, make the tote and zippered purse from the same pair of jeans.

Before assembling the tote bag, sew the pocket onto the cut fabric using a clear thread. Repeat the embroidery process for the change purse by stitching segment 2 and 3 of the Sun before the assembly.

## Towel Trio

Towels make great gifts. These bright colored hand towels are perfect for decorating with the Retro Circle, Retro Square and Retro Triangle. For best results, hoop a piece of tear-away stabilizer, spray the stabilizer with a temporary adhesive and secure the towel to the stabilizer. Embroider the design of choice with a medium weight water-soluble stabilizer. The heavier stabilizer combined with the dense underlay stitches will hold the loops of the towels in place during the embroidery process. Secure all the layers together with segment 1 (perimeter baste) for best results.

## Flutterby

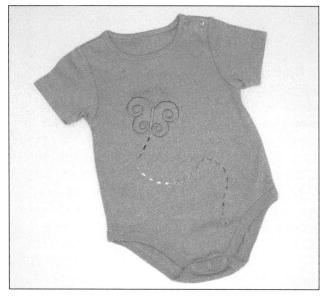

A sewn or purchased onsie makes the perfect canvas to embroider the "Fluttering" Butterfly design. The trick to embroidering on a purchased onsie is to turn it inside out and embroider through the opening in the neck. Hoop a mesh cut-away

stabilizer, spray the stabilizer with adhesive, and secure the front of the onsie onto the stabilizer. The butterfly was randomly placed onto the onsie.

Stitch segment 1 (perimeter baste) to hold the onsie and the stabilizer in place. As the segment 1 and the remainder of the design is stitching, move the onsie neck opening to avoid the fabric from being caught during the embroidery process if necessary.

After the embroidery process, hand sew a random stitching line with variegated needlework thread to represent the flight of the butterfly. For best results use a blunt tip tapestry needle with the smallest eye to accommodate the thicker needlework thread.

## Penny Circle Hat

Dimensional penny circles? With a base fabric of stable organdy, anything is possible! Using the Template Appliqué instructions found on page 9, create templates for the design. Cut the desired size circles from felt using the templates as a guide. Hoop a layer of sheer cream color organdy as the base fabric and stitch the outline segment for the desired size circle. Spray the felt circle piece with a temporary adhesive to secure the circle to the organdy within the stitching. Finish with the coordinating blanket stitch for the circle. A heavier weight cotton thread will help to accentuate the stitching.

## Dimensional Dress

## Snappy Necessity Holder

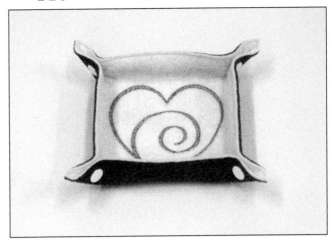

Dimensional cotton print fabric appliques? Sure, with the base fabric made from a stable organdy! Use the instructions from the Penny Circle Hat to form the flowers using the Appliqué Flower design. Trim close to the satin stitch edge and button or snap the flowers into place.

The leaves underneath the dimensional flower at the top of the dress are created from the Flower Spray design and Customizing software or directly on the

embroidery machine. With a larger hoop size, open the Flower Spray design in software or on the embroidery machine. Copy and paste the same design in the hoop in software or open the same design again. Rotate the designs to accommodate the hoop size so the bottom edges of the sprig are close together. Save the design with a new file name before stitching the design onto the project.

What better way to take your embroidery on the road than with a travel accessory that holds personal items, such as rings, watch, necklace and other assorted jewelry. This handy travel essential is made of felt, opens flat for easy transport and can be used on a bedside stand to hold items that you don't want to forget.

Choose two colors of individual felt pieces (that can be found at a local sewing or craft store) to coordinate with a design and thread of your choice. Center and embroider only one felt piece that will be used for the inside of the Necessity Holder. After the embroidery process, use a temporary spray adhesive to secure the two felt pieces together. Mark a 6" square or more around the design. Use a sewing machine to stitch the two layers together directly on the marked square. Trim within 1/8" of the stitching and attach 2 reversible snap closures in each corner according to the manufacturer's instructions.

## Placesetting Pizzazz

Simple, yet coordinating, the addition of an embroidery design at the edge of a cloth napkin can introduce guests to your embroidery creativity. Coordinate fabric cocktail napkins, table runner or coasters with designs to match your dinnerware. With the vast array of designs, thread colors and dinnerware designs, you're sure to come up with some great coordinating ensembles.

For best results, hoop a tear-away stabilizer and spray with a temporary adhesive. Mark the position of the design, align the napkin corner onto the stabilizer, and embroider the design of your choice.

## Penny Circle Play

The Circles (Blanket) were designed to not only show the technique of Template Appliqué, but to use for easy-to-stitch penny circles for quilt projects. Experiment with this technique using brightly colored wool appliqué pieces to make picture frame art (see page 87 in *Embroidery Machine*

*Essentials* for more information on framing).

Make templates of the individual circles in the design using your favorite method and use the templates to plan a design. Mark the fabric using the templates as a guide. Hoop a lightweight tear-away stabilizer, spray the stabilizer with a temporary adhesive, and secure the base fabric into position. Embroider the designs using the Template Appliqué instructions found on page 9.

Here are some ideas for placement that can be used for a wall-hanging, quilt blocks or clothing.

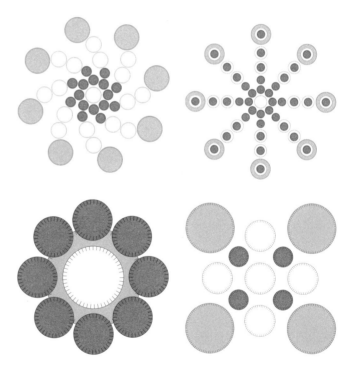

## *Appliqué Curved Square*   Stitch Count: 2,162   Size: 3.17" x 3.52" (80.6mm x 89.5mm)

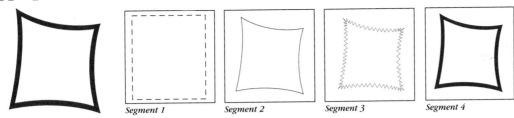

## *Appliqué Flower*   Stitch Count: 3,389   Size: 2.78" x 2.72" (70.7mm x 69.2mm)

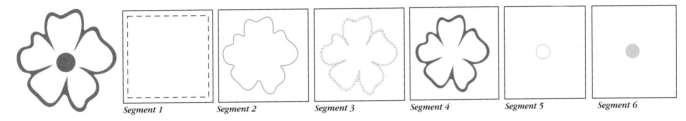

## *Appliqué Leaves & Stem*   Stitch Count: 3,158   Size: 3.68" x 3.20" (93.4mm x 81.4mm)

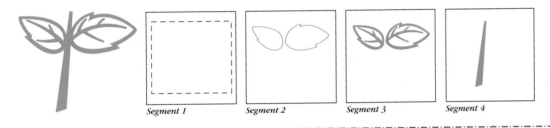

## *Butterfly*   Stitch Count: 5,768   Size: 3.79" x 3.26" (96.2mm x 82.8mm)

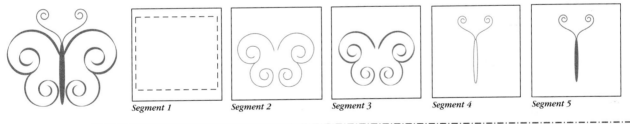

## *Circles – Blanket*   Stitch Count: 2,165   Size: 3.13" x 3.16" (79.6mm x 80.2mm)

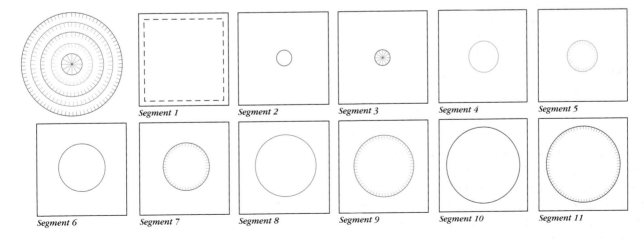

## Circles – Satin   Stitch Count: 5,218   Size: 3.32" x 3.18" (84.2mm x 80.8mm)

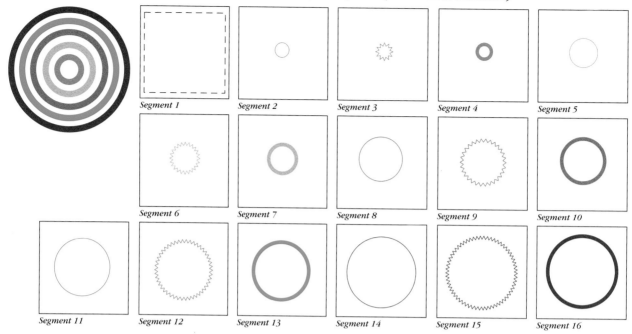

## Cutwork Celtic   Stitch Count: 4,211   Size: 2.71" x 2.66" (68.8mm x 67.6mm)

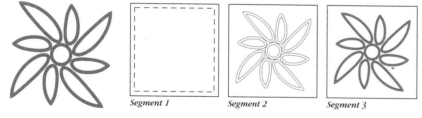

## Cutwork Flower   Stitch Count: 4,935   Size: 3.17" x 3.13" (80.4mm x 79.6mm)

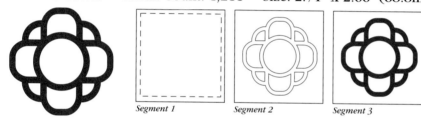

## Cutwork Squares   Stitch Count: 2,886   Size: 2.72" x 2.69" (69.2mm x 68.2mm)

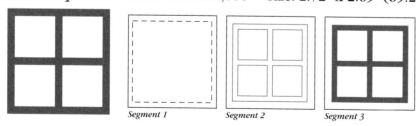

### *Elegant Star*    Stitch Count: 2,039    Size: 3.65" x 3.61" (92.8mm x 91.7mm)

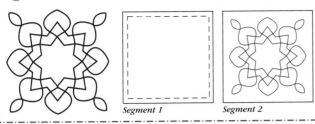

*Segment 1*        *Segment 2*

### *Flower Spray*    Stitch Count: 3,733    Size: 3.47" x 3.39" (88.2mm x 86.2mm)

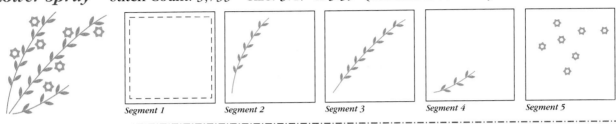

*Segment 1*        *Segment 2*        *Segment 3*        *Segment 4*        *Segment 5*

### *Fringed Flowers*    Stitch Count: 3,178    Size: 3.17" x 3.05" (80.6mm x 77.4mm)

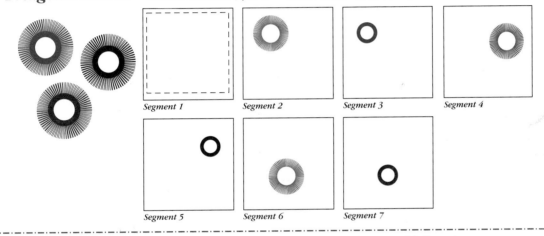

*Segment 1*        *Segment 2*        *Segment 3*        *Segment 4*

*Segment 5*        *Segment 6*        *Segment 7*

### *Heart*    Stitch Count: 3,625    Size: 3.82" x 3.51" (97.0mm x 89.2mm)

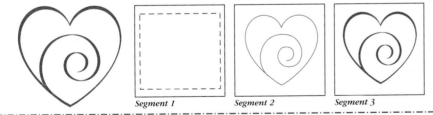

*Segment 1*        *Segment 2*        *Segment 3*

### *Retro Circle*    Stitch Count: 5,218    Size: 2.69" x 3.15" (68.5mm x 80.0mm)

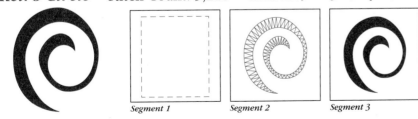

*Segment 1*        *Segment 2*        *Segment 3*

### *Retro Square*    Stitch Count: 7,205    Size: 3.23" x 3.30" (82.0mm x 83.8mm)

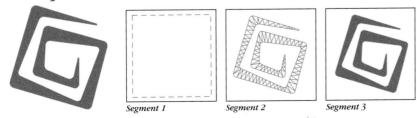

*Segment 1*        *Segment 2*        *Segment 3*

### *Retro Triangle*  Stitch Count: 5,172   Size: 3.08" x 3.04" (78.2mm x 77.2mm)

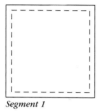
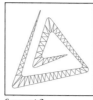

*Segment 1*     *Segment 2*     *Segment 3*

### *Rose – Outline*  Stitch Count: 945   Size: 3.77" x 3.78" (95.7mm x 96.0mm)

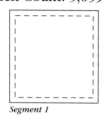

*Segment 1*     *Segment 2*

### *Rose – Satin*  Stitch Count: 5,059   Size: 3.77" x 3.78" (95.7mm x 96.0mm)

*Segment 1*     *Segment 2*

### *Star*  Stitch Count: 6,053   Size: 3.51" x 3.28" (89.2mm x 83.2mm)

*Segment 1*     *Segment 2*     *Segment 3*

### *Sun*  Stitch Count: 5,280   Size: 3.01" x 3.40" (76.4mm x 86.4mm)

*Segment 1*     *Segment 2*     *Segment 3*     *Segment 4*

# Resources

Look for these and other embroidery-related products at your local retailer where embroidery products are sold. Visit www.embroideryresource.com for a comprehensive listing of embroidery machine products.

## Embroidery Machine Companies

### Baby Lock USA
Call 1-800-422-2952 for a dealer near you.
www.babylock.com

### Bernina of America
Call 1-800-405-2739 for a dealer near you.
www.berninausa.com

### Brother International
Call 1-800-422-7684 for a dealer near you.
www.brother.com
www.brothermall.com

### Elna USA
Call 1-800-848-3562 for a dealer near you.
www.elnausa.com

### Janome America
Call 1-800-631-0183 for a dealer near you.
www.janome.com

### Kenmore
1-847-758-0900
www.sears.com

### Pfaff American Sales Corp.
Call 1-800-997-3233 for a dealer near you.
www.pfaffusa.com

### Simplicity
Call 1-800-553-5332 for a dealer near you.
www.simplicitysewing.com

### Singer Company
Call 1-800-474-6437 for a dealer near you.
www.singerco.com

### Viking Sewing Machines
Call 1-800-358-0001 for a dealer near you.
www.husqvarnaviking.com

## Embroidery Design Companies

### Cactus Punch
Call 1-520-622-8460 for a dealer near you.
www.cactuspunch.com

### Criswell Embroidery
Call 1-800-308-5442 for a dealer near you.
www.k-lace.com

### Dakota Collectibles
Call 1-800-331-3160 for a dealer near you.
www.dakotacollectibles.com

### Embroideryarts
Call 1-888-238-1372 for a dealer near you.
www.embroideryarts.com

### Martha Pullen
Call 1-800-547-4176 for a dealer near you.
www.marthapullen.com

### Oklahoma Embroidery Supply & Design (OESD)
See your local sewing & embroidery dealer
Call 1-800-580-8885
www.embroideryonline.com

### Sudberry House
1-860-739-6951
www.machinecrossstitch.com
www.sudberry.com

### Suzanne Hinshaw
1-407-323-8706
www.suzannehinshaw.com

### Vermillion Stitchery
1-949-452-0155
www.vsccs.com

## Other Resources:

### Buzz Tools
www.buzztools.com

### Purrfection (see-through rubberstamps)
www.purrfection.com

### The Snap Source
1-800-725-4600
www.snapsource.com

# Recommended Reading

For more information on embroidery, refer to Jeanine Twigg's books: *Embroidery Machine Essentials*, and her *Project Companion Series: Fleece Techniques* by Nancy Cornwell.

## CD-ROM Instructions

The embroidery designs featured in this book are located on the CD-ROM. You must have a computer and compatible embroidery software to access and utilize the decorative designs. Basic computer knowledge is helpful to understand how to copy the designs onto the hard drive of your computer.

To access the designs, insert the CD-ROM into your computer. The designs are located on the CD-ROM in folders for each embroidery machine format. Copy the design files onto the hard drive of your computer or open the design in applicable embroidery software. Be sure to copy only the design format compatible with your brand of embroidery equipment.

Once the designs are in your embroidery software or saved on your computer, transfer the designs to your embroidery machine following the manufacturer's instructions for the equipment. For more information about using these designs with your software or embroidery equipment, consult your owner's manual or seek advice from the dealer that honors your equipment warranty.

Full-size images of each design with smaller images of the individual segments are included on the CD-ROM in PDF (Portable Document Format) files. In addition, the Appendix: Design Detail (pages 43 - 46) is on the CD-ROM for your convenience. Utilize these pages for design templates and thread color choices.

You will need Adobe Acrobat Reader 5.0 or higher to view and print these files. The CD-ROM includes the latest version of this software for your convenience.